HAL•LEONARD
INSTRUMENTAL
PLAY-ALONG

AUDIO
ACCESS
INCLUDED

PLAYBACK+
Speed • Pitch • Balance • Loop

ALTO SAX

T0081682

Audio arrangements by Peter Deneff

To access audio visit:
www.halleonard.com/mylibrary
Enter Code
5991-6353-7112-2549

ISBN 978-1-5400-2430-5

HAL•LEONARD®
7777 W. BLUEMOUND RD. P.O. BOX 13819 MILWAUKEE, WI 53213

Visit Hal Leonard Online at
www.halleonard.com

BASIN STREET BLUES

ALTO SAX

Words and Music by
SPENCER WILLIAMS

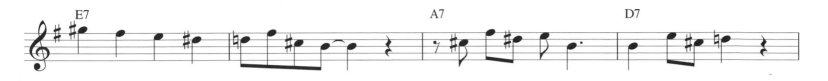

BILL BAILEY,
WON'T YOU PLEASE COME HOME

ALTO SAX

Words and Music by
HUGHIE CANNON

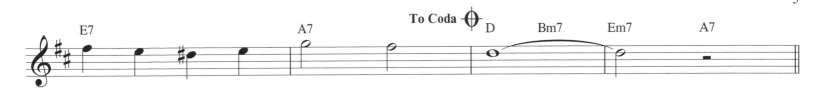

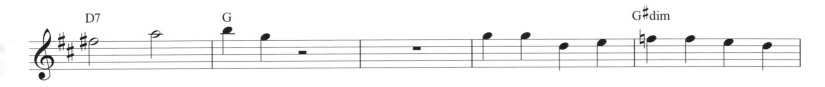

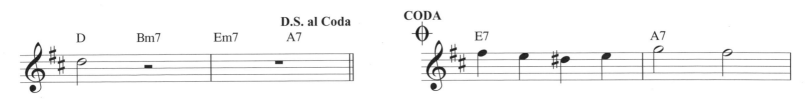

BLACK BOTTOM STOMP

ALTO SAX

By FERD "Jelly Roll" MORTON

BUGLE CALL RAG

ALTO SAX

By HUBERT BLAKE
and CAREY MORGAN

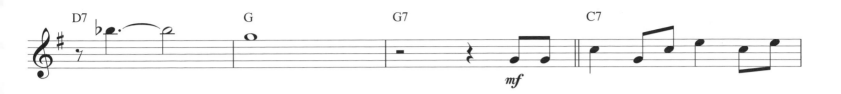

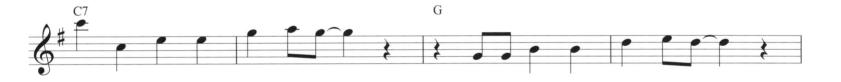

COPENHAGEN

ALTO SAX

Lyric by WALTER MELROSE
Music by CHARLIE DAVIS

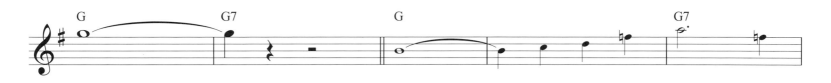

HIGH SOCIETY

ALTO SAX

By PORTER STEELE
and WALTER MELROSE

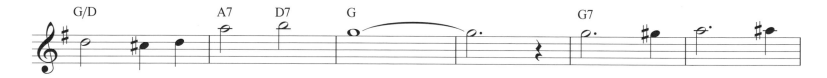

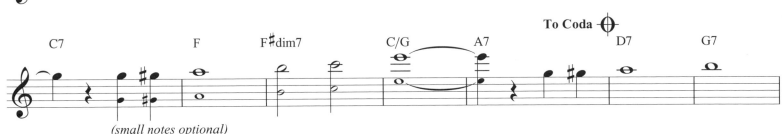

(small notes optional)

MAPLE LEAF RAG

ALTO SAX

Music by SCOTT JOPLIN

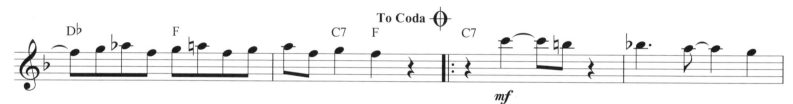

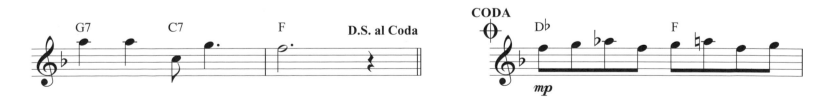

MUSKRAT RAMBLE

ALTO SAX

Written by EDWARD ORY
and RAY GILBERT

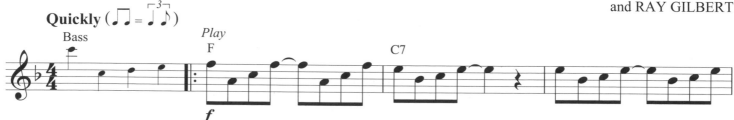

ROYAL GARDEN BLUES

ALTO SAX

Words and Music by CLARENCE WILLIAMS
and SPENCER WILLIAMS

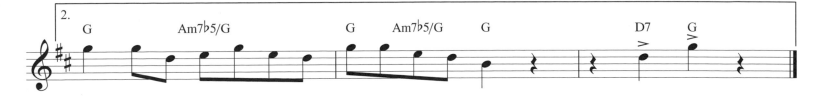

SOUTH RAMPART STREET PARADE

Words by STEVE ALLEN
Music by RAY BAUDUC and BOB HAGGART

ALTO SAX

21

SWEET GEORGIA BROWN

ALTO SAX

Words and Music by BEN BERNIE,
MACEO PINKARD and KENNETH CASEY

23

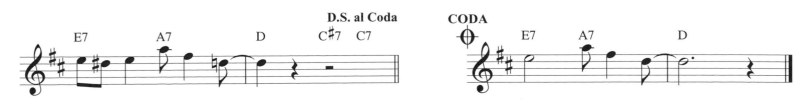

TIGER RAG
(Hold That Tiger)

ALTO SAX

Words by HARRY DeCOSTA
Music by Original Dixieland Jazz Band

TIN ROOF BLUES

ALTO SAX

Lyric by WALTER MELROSE
Music by New Orleans Rhythm Kings

'WAY DOWN YONDER IN NEW ORLEANS

ALTO SAX

Words and Music by HENRY CREAMER
and J. TURNER LAYTON

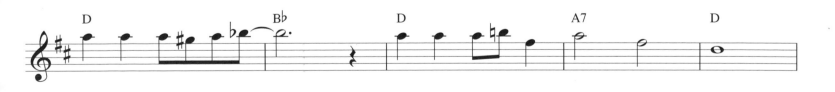

WHEN THE SAINTS GO MARCHING IN

ALTO SAX

Words by KATHERINE E. PURVIS
Music by JAMES M. BLACK

D.S. al Coda
(with repeat)

CODA

HAL·LEONARD INSTRUMENTAL PLAY-ALONG

Your favorite songs are arranged just for solo instrumentalists with this outstanding series. Each book includes a great full-accompaniment play-along audio so you can sound just like a pro! Check out www.halleonard.com to see all the titles available.

The Beatles

All You Need Is Love • Blackbird • Day Tripper • Eleanor Rigby • Get Back • Here, There and Everywhere • Hey Jude • I Will • Let It Be • Lucy in the Sky with Diamonds • Ob-La-Di, Ob-La-Da • Penny Lane • Something • Ticket to Ride • Yesterday.

_____	00225330	Flute	$14.99
_____	00225331	Clarinet	$14.99
_____	00225332	Alto Sax	$14.99
_____	00225333	Tenor Sax	$14.99
_____	00225334	Trumpet	$14.99
_____	00225335	Horn	$14.99
_____	00225336	Trombone	$14.99
_____	00225337	Violin	$14.99
_____	00225338	Viola	$14.99
_____	00225339	Cello	$14.99

Chart Hits

All About That Bass • All of Me • Happy • Radioactive • Roar • Say Something • Shake It Off • A Sky Full of Stars • Someone like You • Stay with Me • Thinking Out Loud • Uptown Funk.

_____	00146207	Flute	$12.99
_____	00146208	Clarinet	$12.99
_____	00146209	Alto Sax	$12.99
_____	00146210	Tenor Sax	$12.99
_____	00146211	Trumpet	$12.99
_____	00146212	Horn	$12.99
_____	00146213	Trombone	$12.99
_____	00146214	Violin	$12.99
_____	00146215	Viola	$12.99
_____	00146216	Cello	$12.99

Coldplay

Clocks • Every Teardrop Is a Waterfall • Fix You • In My Place • Lost! • Paradise • The Scientist • Speed of Sound • Trouble • Violet Hill • Viva La Vida • Yellow.

_____	00103337	Flute	$12.99
_____	00103338	Clarinet	$12.99
_____	00103339	Alto Sax	$12.99
_____	00103340	Tenor Sax	$12.99
_____	00103341	Trumpet	$12.99
_____	00103342	Horn	$12.99
_____	00103343	Trombone	$12.99
_____	00103344	Violin	$12.99
_____	00103345	Viola	$12.99
_____	00103346	Cello	$12.99

Disney Greats

Arabian Nights • Hawaiian Roller Coaster Ride • It's a Small World • Look Through My Eyes • Yo Ho (A Pirate's Life for Me) • and more.

_____	00841934	Flute	$12.99
_____	00841935	Clarinet	$12.99
_____	00841936	Alto Sax	$12.99
_____	00841937	Tenor Sax	$12.95
_____	00841938	Trumpet	$12.99
_____	00841939	Horn	$12.99
_____	00841940	Trombone	$12.99
_____	00841941	Violin	$12.99
_____	00841942	Viola	$12.99
_____	00841943	Cello	$12.99
_____	00842078	Oboe	$12.99

Great Themes

Bella's Lullaby • Chariots of Fire • Get Smart • Hawaii Five-O Theme • I Love Lucy • The Odd Couple • Spanish Flea • and more.

_____	00842468	Flute	$12.99
_____	00842469	Clarinet	$12.99
_____	00842470	Alto Sax	$12.99
_____	00842471	Tenor Sax	$12.99
_____	00842472	Trumpet	$12.99
_____	00842473	Horn	$12.99
_____	00842474	Trombone	$12.99
_____	00842475	Violin	$12.99
_____	00842476	Viola	$12.99
_____	00842477	Cello	$12.99

Popular Hits

Breakeven • Fireflies • Halo • Hey, Soul Sister • I Gotta Feeling • I'm Yours • Need You Now • Poker Face • Viva La Vida • You Belong with Me • and more.

_____	00842511	Flute	$12.99
_____	00842512	Clarinet	$12.99
_____	00842513	Alto Sax	$12.99
_____	00842514	Tenor Sax	$12.99
_____	00842515	Trumpet	$12.99
_____	00842516	Horn	$12.99
_____	00842517	Trombone	$12.99
_____	00842518	Violin	$12.99
_____	00842519	Viola	$12.99
_____	00842520	Cello	$12.99

Songs from Frozen, Tangled and Enchanted

Do You Want to Build a Snowman? • For the First Time in Forever • Happy Working Song • I See the Light • In Summer • Let It Go • Mother Knows Best • That's How You Know • True Love's First Kiss • When Will My Life Begin • and more.

_____	00126921	Flute	$14.99
_____	00126922	Clarinet	$14.99
_____	00126923	Alto Sax	$14.99
_____	00126924	Tenor Sax	$14.99
_____	00126925	Trumpet	$14.99
_____	00126926	Horn	$14.99
_____	00126927	Trombone	$14.99
_____	00126928	Violin	$14.99
_____	00126929	Viola	$14.99
_____	00126930	Cello	$14.99

Top Hits

Adventure of a Lifetime • Budapest • Die a Happy Man • Ex's & Oh's • Fight Song • Hello • Let It Go • Love Yourself • One Call Away • Pillowtalk • Stitches • Writing's on the Wall.

_____	00171073	Flute	$12.99
_____	00171074	Clarinet	$12.99
_____	00171075	Alto Sax	$12.99
_____	00171106	Tenor Sax	$12.99
_____	00171107	Trumpet	$12.99
_____	00171108	Horn	$12.99
_____	00171109	Trombone	$12.99
_____	00171110	Violin	$12.99
_____	00171111	Viola	$12.99
_____	00171112	Cello	$12.99

Wicked

As Long As You're Mine • Dancing Through Life • Defying Gravity • For Good • I'm Not That Girl • Popular • The Wizard and I • and more.

_____	00842236	Flute	$12.99
_____	00842237	Clarinet	$12.99
_____	00842238	Alto Saxophone	$11.95
_____	00842239	Tenor Saxophone	$11.95
_____	00842240	Trumpet	$11.99
_____	00842241	Horn	$12.99
_____	00842242	Trombone	$12.99
_____	00842243	Violin	$11.99
_____	00842244	Viola	$12.99
_____	00842245	Cello	$12.99

Prices, contents, and availability subject to change without notice.
Disney characters and artwork © Disney Enterprises, Inc.